Totes & Bags

LEISURE ARTS, INC. • Maumelle, Arkansas

EDITORIAL STAFF

Vice President of Editorial: Susan White Sullivan

Creative Art Director: Katherine Laughlin

Publications Director: Leah Lampirez

Special Projects Director: Susan Frantz Wiles

Technical Editor: Lisa Lancaster

Technical Assistant: Jean Lewis

Art Category Manager: Lora Puls

Graphic Artists: Becca Snider Tally

Prepress Technician: Stephanie Johnson

Contributing Photographer: Jason Masters

Contributing Photo Stylist: Lori Wenger

BUSINESS STAFF

President and Chief Executive Officer: Rick Barton

Senior Vice President of Operations: Jim Dittrich

Vice President of Finance: Fred F. Pruss

Vice President of Sales-Retail Books: Martha Adams

Vice President of Mass Market: Bob Bewighouse

Vice President of Technology and Planning:
Laticia Mull Dittrich

Controller: Tiffany P. Childers

Information Technology Director: Brian Roden

Director of E-Commerce Services: Mark Hawkins

Manager of E-Commerce: Rob Young

Library of Congress Control Number: 2013952257

ISBN-13: 978-1-4647-1261-6

Meet Sue Marsh

For Sue Marsh of Whistlepig Creek Productions, bags and "smallish quilts" are the kind of projects that drive her passion. "I really enjoy a project that comes together in a short amount of time, as I lose focus quickly. I am always more interested in the next project than the current one."

Sewing from the age of 12, she has loved quick projects since the beginning. "I did my first quilt project from a Quilt in a Day book. I literally made a king-size quilt in a day, and I was hooked."

Sue pursued quilting as a hobby while working in the petroleum industry for 15 years. Then in 1997, she turned to full-time designing of quilt projects and fabrics.

She describes her style as "Random! I like a little bit of everything. My fabric design has been whimsical, with a focus on kids. I've got a couple lines in the works that are modern and good for bag-making."

She still has a soft spot for technology, however.

"I am an engineer by education and a software developer by experience. I love technology and wouldn't/couldn't do my job without software and computerized equipment at my fingertips. The automation takes the tedium out of design and allows me to do the fun stuff."

She especially loves the tools, gadgets, and equipment that are available to quilters. "My house is stuffed with sewing, embroidery, and quilting machines. Plus fabric. Plus thread. Plus patterns. Plus, plus, plus…."

Knowing this about Sue, it's not surprising to hear that her favorite quote is, "If it's worth doing, it's worth doing to excess."

She draws, sews, and quilts at the home she shares with her husband, Bernie, and five cats in a suburb of Denver, Colorado. For more about Sue and Whistlepig Creek Productions, visit her pages on Facebook, Pinterest, and wpcreek.blogspot.com.

With lots of great pockets and styles

that are easy to customize, these 11 fun totes and bags are perfect for all your needs. You'll love the many looks you can create using fat quarters and other pre-cuts or fabric scraps.

Table of Contents

18

38

42

26

32

The Big Easy

This bag un-buttons, un-snaps, and un-zips to expand to a jumbo size to fit all your needs.

Finished Size:
18"w x 12"h x 13"d (46 cm x 30 cm x 33 cm)

SHOPPING LIST

Fabric yardage is based on 43"/44" (109 cm/112 cm) wide fabric with a usable width of 40" (102 cm).

- ☐ 1¼ yds (1.1 m) of fabric #1 for lower linings, inside pockets, outside pockets, end linings, cell phone pockets, and button loop
- ☐ 1⅛ yds (1 m) of fabric #2 for pocket linings (this shows at top of pockets) and handles
- ☐ 1 yd (91 cm) of fabric #3 for bag body, zipper flaps, upper linings, and tab
- ☐ ½ yd (46 cm) of fabric #4 for ends
- ☐ 1½ yds (1.4 m) of 44"/45" (112 cm/114 cm) wide single-sided fusible fleece (such as Pellon® Fusible Thermolam® Plus)
- ☐ 4¾ yds (4.3 m) of 20" (51 cm) wide fusible woven interfacing (such as Pellon® Shape-Flex® SF 101)
- ☐ Large decorative button
- ☐ Two 1⅛" (29 mm) dia buttons
- ☐ ¾" (19 mm) wide hook and loop fastener
- ☐ 16" (41 cm) separating zipper
- ☐ 2 magnetic snaps for ends (You can substitute hook and loop fastener if desired.)
- ☐ Water-soluble fabric marking pen

CUTTING THE PIECES

*Follow **Rotary Cutting**, page 58, **Cutting Chart**, and **Cutting Diagrams**, pages 7-8, to cut fabric. Wof refers to width of fabric. All measurements include ¹/₄" seam allowances.*

Cutting Chart

PIECE(S)	FABRIC	SIZE	CUT
lower lining	#1	18¹/₂" x 14³/₄"	2
inside pocket	#1	18¹/₂" x 7¹/₂"	2
outside pocket	#1	18¹/₂" x 7¹/₂"	2
end lining	#1	pattern, pages 50-51	2
cell phone pocket	#1	5¹/₂" x 12"	2
button loop	#1	8" x 1¹/₂"	1
pocket lining	#2	18¹/₂" x 9¹/₂"	4
handle	#2	5" x wof	3
bag body	#3	18¹/₂" x 16³/₄"	2
zipper flap	#3	17" x 3"	4
upper lining	#3	18¹/₂" x 2¹/₂"	2
tab	#3	pattern, page 50	2
end	#4	pattern, pages 50-51	2
bag body	fusible fleece	33" x 18¹/₂"	1
handle	fusible fleece	5" x wof	3

PIECE(S)	FABRIC	SIZE	CUT
inside pocket	fusible fleece	18¹/₂" x 7¹/₂"	2
end	fusible fleece	pattern, pages 50-51	2
tab	fusible fleece	pattern, page 50	2
bag body	fusible interfacing	18¹/₂" x 16³/₄"	2
lower lining	fusible interfacing	18¹/₂" x 14³/₄"	2
outside pocket	fusible interfacing	18¹/₂" x 7¹/₂"	2
pocket lining	fusible interfacing	18¹/₂" x 9¹/₂"	2
upper lining	fusible interfacing	18¹/₂" x 2¹/₂"	2
zipper flap	fusible interfacing	17" x 3"	4
end	fusible interfacing	pattern, pages 50-51	4
tab	fusible interfacing	pattern, page 50	2

Fabric #1 Cutting Diagram

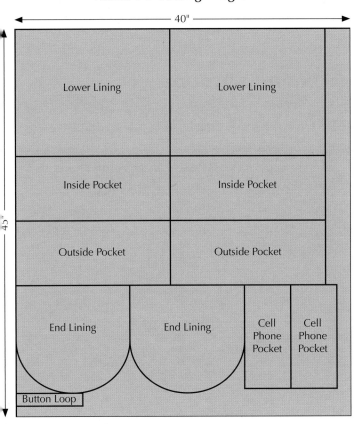

Fabric #3 Cutting Diagram

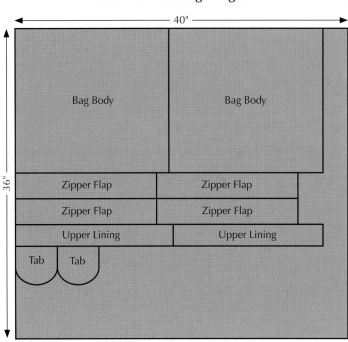

Fabric #2 Cutting Diagram

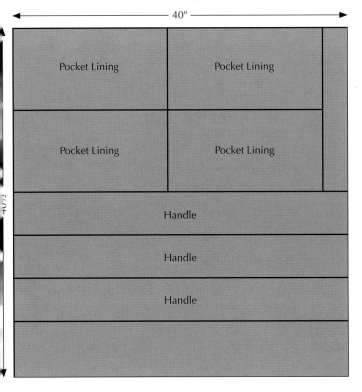

Fusible Fleece Cutting Diagram

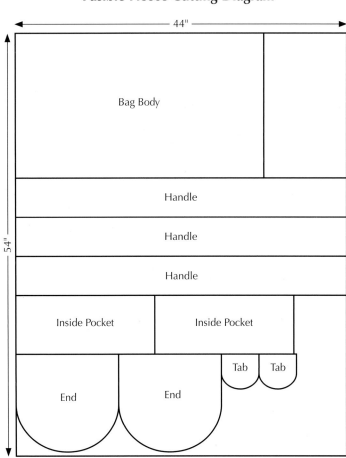

Fusible Interfacing Cutting Diagram

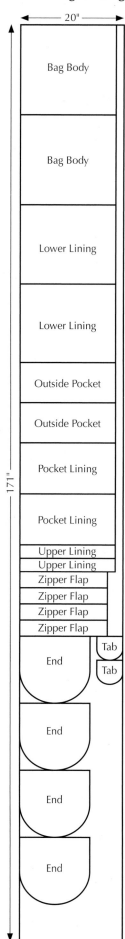

MAKING THE BAG BODY

*Follow **Piecing**, page 59, and **Pressing**, page 60, to make bag. Match right sides and use ¹/₄" seam allowances unless otherwise indicated.*

1. Place fusible side of **fusible interfacing bag body** on wrong side of **bag body**. Follow manufacturer's instructions to fuse. Repeat for remaining bag body.

2. Sew bag bodies together along 1 long edge *(Fig. 1)*. Press seam allowances open.

Fig. 1

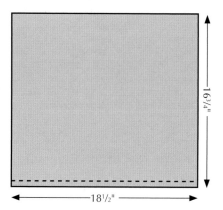

3. Place wrong side of bag body on fusible side of **fusible fleece bag body**. Follow manufacturer's instructions to fuse.

4. Stitch in the ditch through all layers along the seamline.

5. Baste a scant ¹/₄" from all outside edges, through all layers. This helps keep the layers together as you assemble the bag.

MAKING THE OUTSIDE POCKETS

. Place fusible side of **fusible interfacing pocket lining** on wrong side of **pocket lining**; fuse.

. Place fusible side of **fusible interfacing outside pocket** on wrong side of **outside pocket**; fuse.

. Matching long raw edges, sew outside pocket and pocket lining pieces together. Press the seam allowances toward the pocket lining.

. Matching **wrong** sides, align the long raw edges; baste $\frac{1}{8}$" from long edge **(Fig. 2)**. Press flat. The lining will extend about 1" above the outside pocket top.

Fig. 2

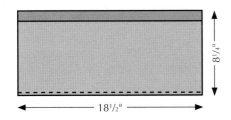

. Stitch in the ditch through all layers along the seamline between the outside pocket and pocket lining.

6. Repeat Steps 1-5 to make remaining outside pocket.

7. Mark a line 11" from each short edge of bag body **(Fig. 3)**.

Fig. 3

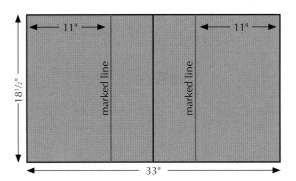

8. Matching right side of outside pocket to right side of bag body, align raw edge of pocket with drawn line **(Fig. 4)**; sew $\frac{1}{4}$" from raw edge. Press outside pocket up. Baste $\frac{1}{8}$" from raw edges. Repeat for remaining outside pocket.

Fig. 4

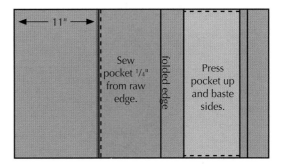

MAKING THE HANDLES

1. Using a diagonal seam *(Fig. 5)*, sew **handles** together end to end. Trim seam allowances to ¼". Press seam allowances open. Trim handle to 120½". Don't worry if yours is slightly shorter.

Fig. 5

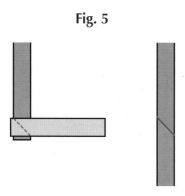

2. Sew ends together diagonally to form a loop.
3. Place the wrong side of handle on the fusible side of **fusible fleece handle**, overlapping ends of fleece slightly. Trim excess fleece; fuse.
4. Matching *wrong* sides, press handle in half; unfold.
5. Press long raw edges of handle to meet the center crease.
6. Matching folded edges, fold handle in half; press.
7. Pin edges together. Sewing through all layers, sew handle close to each edge. Sew additional stitching lines if desired for a decorative effect.

ATTACHING THE HANDLES

1. Mark a line 5" from each long edge of bag body *(Fig. 6)*.

Fig. 6

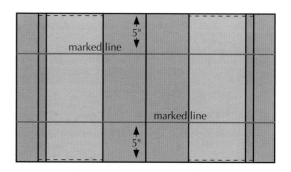

2. Fold handle in half and mark the folds with a straight pin; unfold. Matching pins to bottom seam of bag and handle to drawn line, pin handle to bag body over pockets *(Fig. 7)*.

Fig. 7

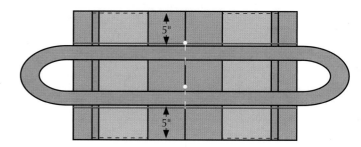

3. Stopping about 2" from top edges of bag body, sew handles close to edge along both sides of handle. Reinforce handles by sewing an "X" *(Fig. 8)*.

Fig. 8

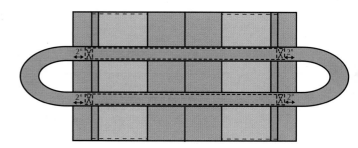

MAKING AND ATTACHING THE BUTTON LOOPS

1. Matching *wrong* sides and long raw edges, press the **button loop** in half; unfold.

2. Matching *wrong* sides, press each long raw edge to meet the center crease.

3. Matching folded edges, fold loop in half on previous crease; press. Pin edges together. Sewing through all layers, sew button loop close to each edge.

4. Cut button loop into two 4" long loops.

5. Matching raw edges, fold one loop in half. Pin one loop to one side edge of bag body 2" from top of bag *(Fig. 9)*. Use a ⅛" seam allowance to sew in place. Repeat with remaining loop.

Fig. 9

MAKING THE TAB

1. Place fusible side of **fusible interfacing tab** on wrong side of **tab**; fuse. Place wrong side of interfaced tab on fusible side of **fusible fleece tab**; fuse. Repeat with remaining tab, interfacing tab, and fusible fleece tab.

2. Sew a 2" length of loop side of hook and loop fastener to 1 tab *(Fig. 10)*.

Fig. 10

3. Leaving straight edges open, sew tabs together. Clip seams and turn tab right side out; press.

4. Topstitch tab ¼" from curved edge. Sew several more stitching lines parallel to the topstitching if desired.

5. Refer to **Fig. 11** to center and sew tab to short edge of bag body on same end as loops with loop fastener facing up. This becomes the bag "back".

Fig. 11

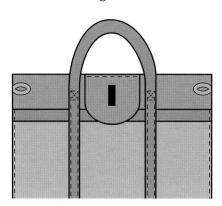

6. With fastener centered side to side and with top 1¼" from the top raw edge of the bag, sew hook side of hook and loop fastener on the bag "front" *(Fig. 12)*.

Fig. 12

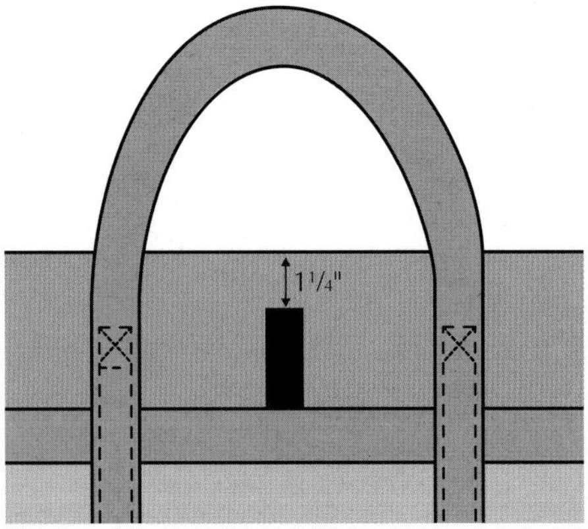

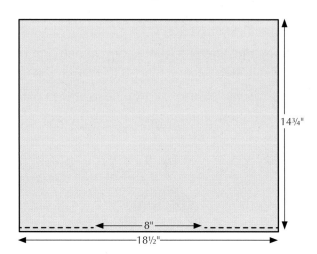

ADDING THE ENDS

1. Transfer snap placement from pattern to right side of fabric on **ends**.
2. Place fusible side of **fusible interfacing end** on wrong side of 1 end; fuse. Place wrong side of interfaced end on fusible side of **fusible fleece end**; fuse.
3. Attach opposite sides of magnetic snap pieces to end where indicated.
4. Mark center of curved edge of end. Matching centers and top edges, pin 1 end to 1 long raw edge of bag body *(Fig. 13)*, clipping the raw edges of the bag body as needed and easing to fit; sew. Press seam allowances toward end. Topstitch very close to seam if desired.

Fig. 13

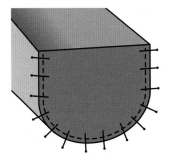

5. Repeat Steps 2-4 for remaining end.

MAKING THE LOWER LINING

1. Place the **lower lining interfacing** on the wrong side of the **lower lining**; fuse. Repeat for remaining lower lining.
2. Sew lower linings together across 1 long edge *(Fig. 14)*, leaving a large opening (8") for turning. Press seam allowances open.

Fig. 14

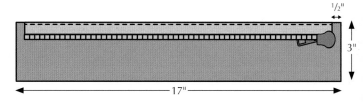

MAKING THE ZIPPER FLAPS

1. Place the **zipper flap interfacing** on the wrong side of 1 **zipper flap**; fuse. Repeat for remaining zipper flaps.
2. Un-zip the zipper.
3. Matching right sides, center 1 half of zipper on the right side of 1 zipper flap with edge of zipper tape aligned with raw edge of zipper flap. Sew a scant ¼" from raw edge of zipper flap *(Fig. 15)*.

Fig. 15

Unbutton it.

Unsnap it.

Unzip it.

4. With zipper half sandwiched in between and matching right sides and raw edges of flaps, place a second flap on the first flap. Sew over the same stitching line sewn in previous step.

5. Using a ¼" seam allowance, sew ends of flaps *(Fig. 16)*. Clip corners and turn right side out; press. Topstitch along zipper flap *(Fig. 17)*.

Fig. 16

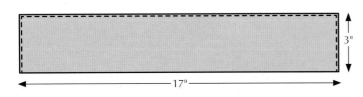

Fig. 17

6. Repeat Steps 3-5 with remaining zipper flaps and corresponding zipper piece.

SEWING THE ZIPPER FLAPS TO THE LOWER LINING

1. Place the **upper lining interfacing** on the wrong side of 1 **upper lining**; fuse. Repeat for remaining upper lining.

2. Mark a dot 1" from sides of lower lining along each short edge *(Fig. 18)*. With **wrong** side of zipper flap against right side on 1 short edge of lower lining, place zipper flap between dots. Sew in place with a scant ¼" seam. Repeat for remaining short edge of lower lining.

Fig. 18

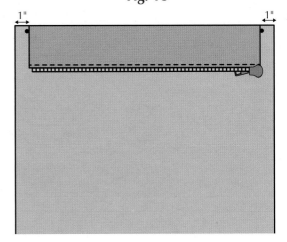

3. With zipper flap sandwiched in between and matching right sides and raw edges, place 1 upper lining on 1 lower lining. Sew in place. Open and press upper lining up. Press seam allowances toward lower lining. Repeat with remaining upper lining on opposite edge of lower lining.

TIP
Don't love zippers? Substitute hook and loop fastener! Sew the flaps together as above and then sew 1 length of hook and loop fastener to the top side of 1 flap and to the bottom side of the other flap so the pieces overlap.

MAKING THE INSIDE POCKETS

. Matching long raw edges, sew 1 **inside pocket** and 1 **pocket lining** together. Press seam allowances toward pocket lining.

. Matching **wrong** sides, align long raw edges; press. The lining will extend about 1" above the pocket.

. Open pocket and align 1 long edge of **inside pocket fleece** against pressed crease. Fold pocket closed and fuse.

. Baste pocket $1/8$" from long raw edge **(Fig. 19)**.

Fig. 19

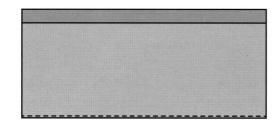

. Stitch in the ditch through all layers between the pocket and lining.

. Repeat Steps 1-5 for remaining inside pocket.

SEWING THE INSIDE POCKETS TO THE LINING

1. Mark a line 11" from each short edge of lining **(Fig. 20)**.

Fig. 20

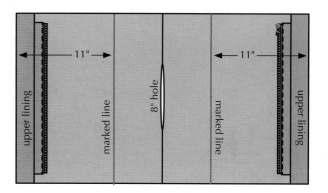

2. Matching right side of inside pocket to right side of lining, align raw edge of pocket with drawn line *(Fig. 21)*; sew. Press inside pocket up. Baste ¹/₈" from each side. Be sure to move zipper flaps out of the way.

Fig. 21

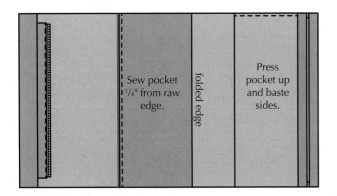

3. Sew a vertical dividing line down center of inner pocket to create pockets or divide as you desire.

4. Repeat Steps 2-3 for remaining pocket.

MAKING THE CELL PHONE POCKET

1. Matching right sides, fold cell phone pocket in half to make a 5¹/₂" x 6" piece. Sew along 6" sides *(Fig. 22)*. Clip corners and turn right sides out; press.

Fig. 22

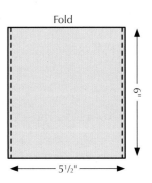

2. Fuse 1 **fusible interfacing end** to wrong side of 1 **end lining**.

3. On right side of fabric, draw a horizontal line 8" from top across end lining. Center raw edges of pocket along drawn line with folded side of pocket pointing down *(Fig. 23)*. Sew ¹/₄" from raw edge.

Fig. 23

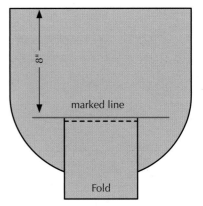

Press pocket up and topstitch along sides and bottom (*Fig. 24*).

Fig. 24

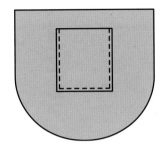

Repeat Steps 1-4 for remaining cell phone pocket.

ADDING THE LINING ENDS

Refer to **Adding the Ends**, page 12, Step 4, to sew end lining to lining.

ASSEMBLING THE BAG

Matching right sides, place the bag inside the lining. Matching seams, sew raw edges together around top (*Fig. 25*).

Fig. 25

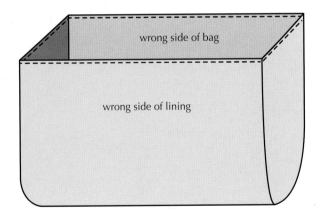

wrong side of bag

wrong side of lining

2. Turn bag right sides out through opening. Hand stitch opening closed. Push lining into bag. Folding handles out of the way, topstitch around top of bag if desired.

3. Catching handles in stitching, topstitch upper lining to bag on front and back just above the zipper flap (*Fig. 26*) through all layers. This stitching will show on right side of bag. Sew small buttons to ends of bag front over topstitching. Sew large decorative button to tab.

Fig. 26

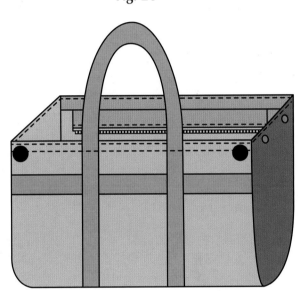

3 Charming Totes

This pattern is designed to utilize charm squares. All the totes have a cute cuff on the outside, pockets on the inside, and an optional drawstring closure. The pattern also gives you 3 options for the front and back of the tote. One tote features a little pocket, perfect for your cell phone, one tote features charm squares turned on point, and one tote features dimensional pinwheels.

Finished Size:
13½"w x 13½"h x 4½"d (34 cm x 34 cm x 11 cm)

SHOPPING LIST

Fabric yardage is based on 43"/44" (109 cm/112 cm) wide fabric with a usable width of 40" (102 cm). Fat quarters measure approximately 21" x 18" (53 cm x 46 cm). Charm squares measure 5" x 5" (13 cm x 13 cm).

For all totes:
- ☐ ¼ yd (23 cm) of fabric #1 **or** 1 fat quarter for cuff
- ☐ ⅞ yd (80 cm) of fabric #2 for lining and inside pocket
- ☐ 1 yd (91 cm) of fusible interfacing (such as Pellon® Shape-Flex® SF 101)
- ☐ ⅞ yd (80 cm) of fusible fleece (such as Pellon® Fusible Thermolam® Plus)
- ☐ ⅜ yd (34 cm) of fabric #3 **or** 1 fat quarter for drawstring closure (optional)
- ☐ 2 yds (1.8 m) of cord or ribbon for drawstring (optional)
- ☐ water-soluble fabric marking pen

For Pocket Tote, you will also need:
- ☐ 41 charm squares for front, back, sides, bottom, and handle*
- ☐ Eight ⁹⁄₁₆" (14 mm) dia. buttons

For Charms-On-Point Tote, you will also need:
- ☐ 37 charm squares for front, back, sides, bottom, and handle*
- ☐ ⅜ yd (34 cm) of accent fabric
- ☐ Eight ⁹⁄₁₆" (14 mm) dia. buttons

For Pinwheel Tote, you will also need:
- ☐ 45 charm squares for front, back, sides, bottom, and handle*
- ☐ Two 1⅛" (29 mm) dia. buttons

*A fat quarter can be substituted for 9 charm squares for the sides and bottom of the tote.

Pocket Tote

Charms-On-Point Tote

Pinwheel Tote

19

CUTTING THE PIECES

*Follow **Rotary Cutting**, page 58, **Cutting Charts**, and **Cutting Diagram**, to cut fabric. All measurements include ¹/₄" seam allowances.*

Cutting Chart (for all totes)

PIECE(S)	FABRIC	SIZE	CUT
cuff	#1	18¹/₂" x 7"	2
lining	#2	18¹/₂" x 16¹/₄"	2
inside pocket	#2	18¹/₂" x 12"	2
lining	fusible interfacing	18¹/₂" x 16¹/₄"	2
front/back	fusible fleece	14" x 14"	2
side/bottom	fusible fleece	14" x 5"	3
cuff	fusible fleece	18¹/₂" x 3"	2
handle	fusible fleece*	23" x 5"	2
drawstring closure (optional)	#3	18¹/₂" x 9"	2

*The handles are quite thick. You may choose to use interfacing or a lighter weight fleece for the handles.

Cutting Chart (for Charms-On-Point Tote)

PIECE(S)	FABRIC	SIZE	CUT
short sashing	accent fabric	1" x 5"	12
long sashing	accent fabric	1" x 15"	4
corners	accent fabric	7" x 7"	2

Fusible Fleece Cutting Diagram

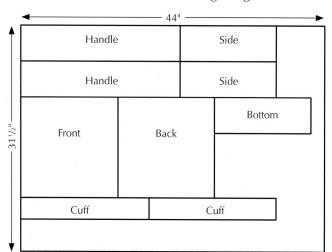

MAKING THE FRONT AND BACK

*Follow the instructions for your desired tote front and back. Follow **Piecing**, page 59, and **Pressing**, page 60, to make tote. Match right sides and use ¹/₄" seam allowances unless otherwise indicated.*

Pocket Tote

1. For pocket, sew 2 assorted **charm squares** together along 1 edge. Turn right side out; press.
2. Press sewn edge down 1".
3. Place pocket on 1 square and baste in place ¹/₈" from sides and bottom to make **Unit 1**. Make 2 Unit 1's.

Unit 1 (make 2)

4. Sew 3 assorted charm squares together to make **Unit 2**. Make 4 Unit 2's.

Unit 2 (make 4)

5. Sew 1 assorted charm square on each side of Unit 1 to make **Unit 3**. Make 2 Unit 3's.

Unit 3 (make 2)

6. Sew 2 Unit 2's and 1 Unit 3 together to make **front**. Repeat to make **back**.

Front/Back

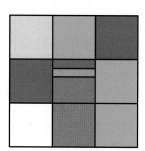

Charms-On-Point Tote

1. Sew 2 **short sashings** and 3 assorted charm squares together to make **Unit 4**. Make 6 Unit 4's.

Unit 4 (make 6)

2. Sew 2 **long sashings** and 3 Unit 4's together to make **Unit 5**. Make 2 Unit 5's.

Unit 5 (make 2)

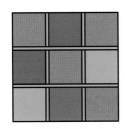

3. Cut each **corner** *twice* diagonally *(Fig. 1)* to make 8 **corner triangles**.

Fig. 1

4. Center and sew long edges of corner triangles to sides of Unit 5 *(Fig. 2)*. Press triangles outward *(Fig. 3)*. The triangles are oversized and will be trimmed later.

Fig. 2   **Fig. 3**

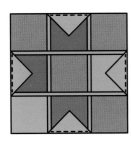

5. Rotate piece 45°. Trimming an even amount from all sides, trim piece to a square 14" x 14" *(Fig. 4)* to make **front**.

Fig. 4   **Front**

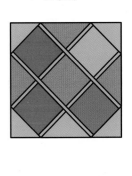

6. Repeat Steps 4-5 to make **back**.

Pinwheel Tote

1. Fold 1 charm square to make a **Prairie Point**. Make 8 Prairie Points.

Prairie Point (make 8)

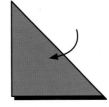

2. Sew 1 Prairie Point to 1 charm square to make a **Prairie Point Square**. Make 8 Prairie Point Squares. Trim triangle points even with sides of charm square to eliminate bulk.

Prairie Point Square (make 8)

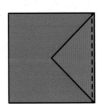

3. Sew 2 Prairie Point Squares together to make **Unit 6**. Make 4 Unit 6's. Press seam allowances open.

Unit 6 (make 4)

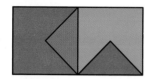

4. Sew 2 Unit 6's together to make a **Prairie Point Block**. Stitch across intersection again to reinforce the center seam. Pick out a couple of stitches in the seam allowances to allow the seam allowances to lie in opposite directions. Make 2 Prairie Point Blocks.

Prairie Point Block (make 2)

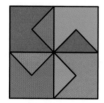

5. Sew 2 charm squares together to make **Unit 7**. Make 2 Unit 7's.

Unit 7 (make 2)

6. Sew 1 Unit 7 to left side of Prairie Point Block to make **Unit 8**. Make 2 Unit 8's.

Unit 8 (make 2)

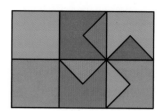

7. Sew 3 charm squares together to make **Unit 9**. Make 2 Unit 9's.

Unit 9 (make 2)

8. Sew 1 Unit 9 to 1 Unit 8 to make **front**. Repeat to make **back**.

Front/Back

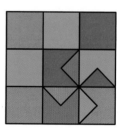

MAKING THE SIDES AND BOTTOM

1. Sew 3 charm squares together to make 1 **side**. Repeat to make another side and 1 **bottom**. You may substitute 3 rectangles 5" x 14", cut from fat quarters.

MAKING THE HANDLES

1. Sew 5 charm squares together side by side to make 1 **handle**.
2. Follow manufacturer's instructions to fuse the wrong side of 1 handle on the fusible side of 1 **fusible fleece handle**. Repeat for remaining handle.
3. Matching **wrong** sides and long edges, press handle in half; unfold.
4. Press long raw edges of handle to meet the center crease.
5. Matching folded edges, fold handle in half; press.
6. Pin edges together. Sewing through all layers, sew handle close to each edge. Sew additional stitching lines if desired for a decorative effect.
7. Repeat Steps 1-6 for remaining handle.

MAKING THE CUFF

1. Matching **wrong** sides, fold **cuff** in half lengthwise; press.
2. Unfold the cuff and place the fusible side of the **cuff fleece** on the wrong side of the fabric, aligning 1 long edge of the fleece with the fold of the fabric. Refold the cuff and fuse fleece in place.
3. Repeat Steps 1-2 to make a second cuff.
4. Unfold the cuff pieces again. Matching fleece-covered areas, sew short edges together. Press seam allowances open. Refold the cuff.

Optional Drawstring Closure

MAKING THE DRAWSTRING CLOSURE (OPTIONAL FOR ALL TOTES)

1. Beginning 2" from edge (top) on one end only, sew **drawstring closure** pieces together along short sides *(Fig. 5)*.

Fig. 5

2" [

2. Press the seam allowances open, pressing the unsewn area 1/4" to wrong side.
3. To form casing, fold top edge 1/4" to inside; press 1" to inside again. Sew close to each folded edge.

MAKING THE LINING AND INSIDE POCKETS

1. Matching **wrong** sides, fold 1 **inside pocket** in half lengthwise so that pocket is 6" x 18½". Repeat with remaining inside pocket.
2. Place the fusible side of 1 **fusible interfacing lining** on the wrong side of 1 **lining**. Follow manufacturer's instructions to fuse.
3. Draw a horizontal line across lining 3" from 1 long edge of tote (bottom).

4. With folded edge of inside pocket pointing downward, match raw edges of pocket to drawn line *(Fig. 6)*; pin. Sew pocket in place ¹/₄" from edge.

Fig. 6

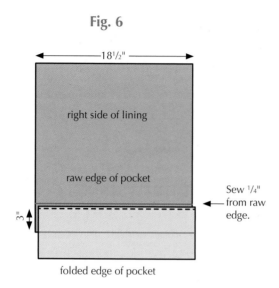

right side of lining

raw edge of pocket

18¹/₂"

3"

Sew ¹/₄" from raw edge.

folded edge of pocket

5. Press pocket up and baste at each side. Sew vertical lines to create pocket dividers *(Fig. 7)*.

Fig. 7

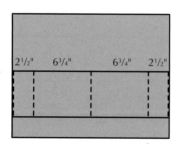

2¹/₂" 6³/₄" 6³/₄" 2¹/₂"

6. Refer to **Fig. 8** to cut a 2¹/₄" notch from each bottom corner.

Fig. 8

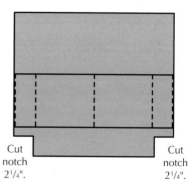

Cut notch 2¹/₄".

Cut notch 2¹/₄".

7. Repeat Steps 2-6 to make remaining lining piece.

8. Matching pockets and leaving a 6" opening for turning, sew lining pieces together along each side and the bottom **(Fig. 9)**.

Fig. 9

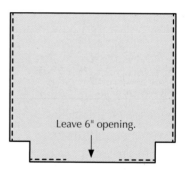

Leave 6" opening.

9. To box the bottom, match right sides and align side seam with bottom seam; sew across ends **(Fig. 10)**.

Fig. 10

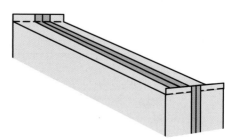

ASSEMBLING THE TOTE

1. Place wrong side of tote front on fusible side of **fusible fleece front**; fuse. Topstitch around each square, if desired. Repeat with tote back.

2. Sew buttons to tote front and back.

3. Place wrong side of **bottom** on fusible side of **fusible fleece bottom**; fuse. Topstitch around each square, if desired. If using a rectangle instead of charm squares, quilt as desired. Repeat with each side.

4. Stopping and backstitching $1/4$" from bottom edge, sew sides to front of tote.

5. Stopping and backstitching $1/4$" from bottom edge, sew sides to back of tote.

6. Stopping and backstitching $1/4$" from each corner, sew bottom to front, back, and sides of tote.

7. Trim corners and turn tote right side out.

8. Matching raw edges and side seams, sew cuff to right side of tote body.

9. Pin raw edges of 1 handle even with top edge and 6" from side seams over cuff (*Fig. 11*); baste in place. Sew again to reinforce seam. Repeat for remaining handle on tote back.

Fig. 11

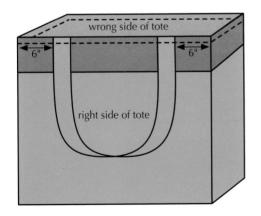

10. If adding drawstring closure, match raw edges and sew right side of **drawstring closure** to right side of tote body with cuff and handles sandwiched in between.

11. Matching right sides, place tote body into lining with cuff, handle, and optional drawstring closure sandwiched in between. Aligning top raw edges and side seams, stitch around top (*Fig. 12*).

Fig. 12

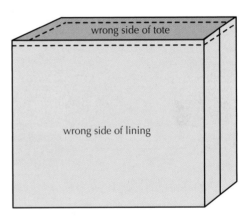

12. Turn tote right side out through the opening in the lining. Hand stitch opening closed. Tuck lining and optional drawstring closure into tote. Turn cuff up out of the way. Topstitch around top of tote. The handles are thick; sew slowly to avoid breaking the needle.

13. Thread drawstring through casing.

OPTIONAL STURDY BOTTOM

Cut 2 pieces of mat board $4^1/2$" x $13^1/2$"; glue together. Cut two $5^1/4$" x $14^1/4$" fabric pieces. Matching right sides, place fabric pieces together. Sew along 2 long edges and 1 short edge; turn right side out. Press raw edges $1/4$" to wrong side; press $1/4$" to wrong side again. Insert mat board into case. To close, stitch along folded edges.

The Big Shopper

Instructions are given for 3 larger bags and 3 smaller bags.
You can choose from a variety of widths, heights, and depths.
The pattern also gives you 3 options for the front and back of the bag.
Strips or charm squares can be substituted for the solid front and back.

FINISHED SIZES

LARGER BAGS		SMALLER BAGS	
Ⓐ	18½"w x 15"h x 4½"d (47 cm x 38 cm x 11 cm)	**Ⓓ**	16½"w x 15"h x 4½"d (42 cm x 38 cm x 11 cm)
Ⓑ	17"w x 16"h x 6"d (43 cm x 41 cm x 15 cm)	**Ⓔ**	15"w x 16"h x 6"d (38 cm x 41 cm x 15 cm)
Ⓒ	14"w x 14½"h x 9"d (36 cm x 37 cm x 23 cm)	**Ⓕ**	12"w x 14½"h x 9"d (30 cm x 37 cm x 23 cm)

SHOPPING LIST

Yardage is based on 43"/44" (109 cm/112 cm) wide fabric with a usable width of 40" (102 cm).

☐ ⅜ yd (34 cm) of fabric #1 for top band
☐ ⅛ yd (11 cm) of fabric #2 for accent strip
☐ 12" x 12" (30 cm x 30 cm) square of fabric #3 for circle
☐ ⅞ yd (80 cm) of fabric #4 for bag body*
☐ 5" x 10" (13 cm x 25 cm) piece of fabric #5 for letter appliqués
☐ 1½ yds (1.4 m) of fabric #6 for lining and inside pockets (If using directional fabric, you will need 2 yds [1.8 m].)
☐ ¼ yd (23 cm) of fabric #7 for handle**
☐ 2 yds (1.8 m) of 44"/45" (112 cm/114 cm) wide single-sided fusible fleece (such as The Warm Company® Warm Fleece™ or Pellon® #987F)
☐ Sixteen ⅝" (16 mm) buttons (optional, if using charm squares)
☐ Paper-backed fusible web
☐ Stabilizer
☐ Water-soluble fabric marking pen

* Twelve assorted 2½" (6.35 cm) wide strips or 30 assorted 5" x 5" (12.7 cm x 12.7 cm) charm squares can be substituted for the bag body fabric.
**22 assorted rectangles 2½" x 5" (6.35 cm x 12.7 cm) can be substituted for the handle fabric.

CUTTING THE PIECES

*Follow **Rotary Cutting**, page 58, and **Cutting Charts**, to cut fabric. Wof refers to width of fabric. All measurements include $1/4$" seam allowances.*

Cutting Chart (Larger Bags)

PIECE(S)	FABRIC	SIZE	CUT
top band	#1	23" x 5"	2
accent strip	#2	23" x $1^1/2$"	2
circle	#3	use circle pattern, page 52	4
bag body	#4	23" x 14" **or** 5" x 5" charm squares **or** strips $2^1/2$"w x wof	2 30 12
lining	#6	23" x $19^1/2$"	2
inside pocket	#6	23" x 12"	2
handle	#7	5" x wof **or** rectangles $2^1/2$" x 5"	1 22
bag body	fusible fleece	23" x $19^1/2$"	4
handle	fusible fleece	5" x wof	1
inside pocket	fusible fleece	23" x $5^1/2$"	2
circle	fusible fleece	use circle pattern, page 52	2

Cutting Chart (Smaller Bags)

PIECE(S)	FABRIC	SIZE	CUT
top band	#1	21" x 5"	2
accent strip	#2	21" x $1^1/2$"	2
circle	#3	use circle pattern, page 52	4
bag body	#4	21" x 14" **or** 5" x 5" charm squares **or** strips $2^1/2$"w x wof	2 30 12
lining	#6	21" x $19^1/2$"	2
inside pocket	#6	21" x 12"	2
handle	#7	5" x wof **or** rectangles $2^1/2$" x 5"	1 22
bag body	fusible fleece	21" x $19^1/2$"	4
handle	fusible fleece	5" x wof	1
inside pocket	fusible fleece	21" x $5^1/2$"	2
circle	fusible fleece	use circle pattern, page 52	2

CUTTING THE APPLIQUÉS

From fabric #5 for letter appliqué:

• Find a font you like on the computer. Size desired letter to approximately $3^1/2$" tall; print. Using printed letter for pattern, refer to **Preparing Fusible Appliqués**, page 60, to cut desired **letter**.

HELPFUL MEASUREMENTS

Use the following measurements to determine the size to cut the corner notch for boxing the bag bottom, the placement of the inside pockets, and what size to make the optional sturdy bottom for the various size bags.

FINISHED BAG SIZE	NOTCH SIZE	POCKET ALIGNMENT LINE	BAG BOTTOM SIZE
Larger Bags			
Ⓐ 18¹/₂"w x 15"h x 4¹/₂"d	2¹/₄" x 2¹/₄"	16¹/₄" from top	18¹/₂" x 4¹/₂"
Ⓑ 17"w x 16"h x 6"d	3" x 3"	15¹/₂" from top	17" x 6"
Ⓒ 14"w x 14¹/₂"h x 9"d	4¹/₂" x 4¹/₂"	14" from top	14" x 9"
Smaller Bags			
Ⓓ 16¹/₂"w x 15"h x 4¹/₂"d	2¹/₄" x 2¹/₄"	16¹/₄" from top	16¹/₂" x 4¹/₂"
Ⓔ 15"w x 16"h x 6"d	3" x 3"	15¹/₂" from top	15" x 6"
Ⓕ 12"w x 14¹/₂"h x 9"d	4¹/₂" x 4¹/₂"	14" from top	12" x 9"

MAKING THE BAG BODY

Follow Piecing, page 59, and Pressing, page 60, using the pieces cut for your desired size bag. Dimensions for smaller sizes are shown in parentheses. Match right sides and use ¹/₄" seam allowances unless otherwise indicated.

1. There are 3 options for the bag body. The **bag body** given in the cutting list can be used or the bag body can be pieced from charm squares or strips.

   If using charm squares for bag body, sew 5 **charm squares** together to make a row. Make 3 Rows. Sew the rows together to make a 23" x 14" bag body front for larger bags. For smaller bags, trim the rectangle to 21" x 14". Repeat for bag body back of corresponding size.

   If using strips for bag body, sew 12 **strips** together along long edges. From this piece, cut 2 rectangles 23" x 14" (21" x 14") for bag body front and back.

2. Refer to **Fig. 1** to sew 1 top band, 1 accent strip, and 1 bag body front together to make bag front.

Fig. 1

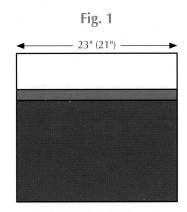

23" (21")

3. Place wrong side of bag front on fusible side of **fusible fleece bag body**. Follow manufacturer's instructions to fuse. If desired, topstitch along each seamline or around each square through all layers. For charm square bag, sew 1 button at the intersection of each group of 4 squares.

4. Repeat Steps 2-3 to make bag back.

5. Center and fuse 1 letter on 1 **fabric circle**. Refer to **Machine Applique**, page 60, to stitch letter in place using a narrow satin stitch or a blanket stitch.

6. Place wrong side of letter circle on fusible side of **fusible fleece circle**; fuse.

7. Cut a 2" slit in the center of another fabric circle.

8. Matching right sides, layer letter circle and slit circle together. Sew around outer edge of circles. Turn circle right side out through slit; press.

9. Refer to **Fig. 2** to position circle on bag front; pin. Sew circle in place using a narrow satin stitch or a blanket stitch.

Fig. 2

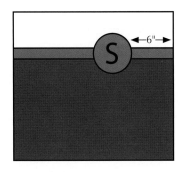

6"

10. Repeat Steps 5-9 to sew circle to bag back.

11. Referring to **Helpful Measurements** to determine notch size, cut a notch *(Fig. 3)* from each bottom corner of front and back.

Fig. 3

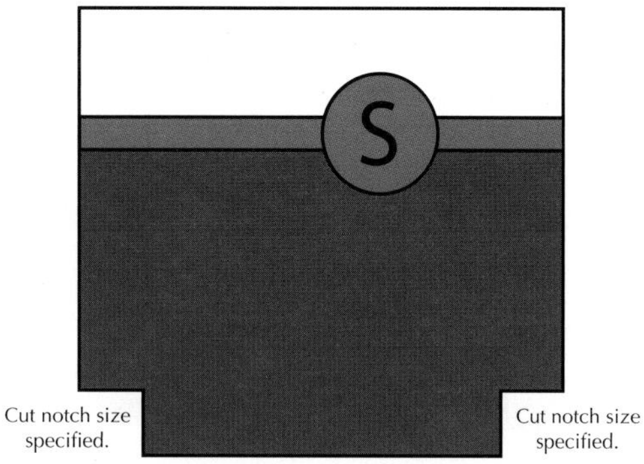

Cut notch size specified.   Cut notch size specified.

12. Sew front and back together along each side and the bottom.

13. To box the bottom, match right sides and align side seams with bottom seam; sew across ends *(Fig. 4)*.

Fig. 4

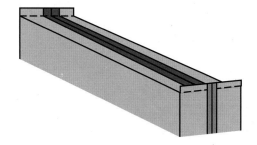

MAKING AND ATTACHING THE HANDLES

1. There are 2 options for the handles. The handles can be made from a single strip or from assorted small fabric pieces.
   If using assorted small fabric pieces, match long edges and sew 22 **rectangles** together to make a handle.

2. Place the wrong side of handle on the fusible side of **fusible fleece handle**; fuse.

3. Matching **wrong** sides, press handle in half; unfold. Press long raw edges of handle to meet center crease.

4. Matching folded edges, fold handle in half; press.

5. Pin edges together. Sewing through all layers, sew handle close to each edge. Sew additional stitching lines if desired for a decorative effect.

6. Cut handle in half to make 2 handles.

7. Pin raw edges of 1 handle even with top edge and 7½" (6½") from side seams on right side of bag back *(Fig. 5)*; baste in place. Repeat for remaining handle on bag front.

Fig. 5

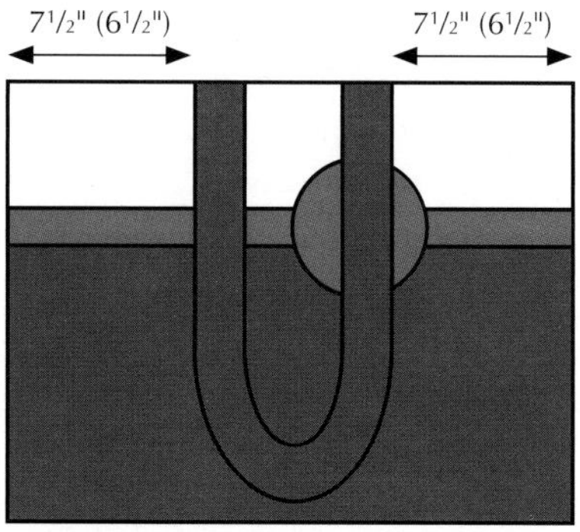

7½" (6½")   7½" (6½")

MAKING THE INSIDE POCKETS

1. Matching wrong sides, fold **inside pocket** in half lengthwise so that pocket is 23" (21") x 6".

2. Unfold the pocket and place the fusible side of the corresponding **fusible fleece inside pocket** on the wrong side of the fabric, aligning 1 long edge of the fleece with the fold of the fabric. Refold the pocket and fuse fleece in place.

3. Repeat Steps 1-2 to make another inside pocket.

MAKING THE LINING

1. Place the wrong side of 1 **lining** on the fusible side of 1 **fusible fleece bag body** and fuse.

2. Refer to **Helpful Measurements** to draw pocket alignment line across lining parallel with top edge of bag. With folded edge of inside pocket pointing downward, match raw edges of pocket to drawn line *(Fig. 6)*; pin. Sew pocket in place 1/4" from edge.

Fig. 6

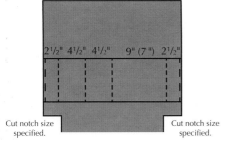

3. Press pocket up and baste at each side. Sew vertical lines to create pocket dividers *(Fig. 7)*. Referring to **Helpful Measurements** to determine notch size, cut a notch from each bottom corner of front and back lining.

Fig. 7

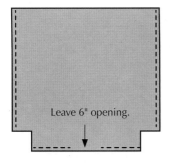

4. Repeat Steps 1-3 to make remaining lining piece.
5. Matching pockets and leaving a 6" opening for turning, sew lining pieces together along each side and the bottom *(Fig. 8)*.

Fig. 8

Leave 6" opening.

6. To box the bottom, match right sides and align side seam with bottom seam; sew across ends *(see Fig. 4)*.

ASSEMBLING THE BAG

1. Matching right sides, place the bag inside the lining with the handle sandwiched in between. Aligning top raw edges and matching side seams, sew raw edges together around top *(Fig. 9)*.

Fig. 9

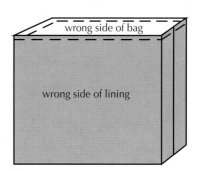

2. Turn bag right side out through opening. Hand stitch opening closed. Push lining into bag. Topstitch around top of bag if desired.

OPTIONAL STURDY BOTTOM

Refer to **Helpful Measurements** to cut 2 pieces of mat board the size of the bag bottom - 1/2"; glue together. Cut two pieces of scrap fabric the size of the bag bottom + 1/2". Matching right sides, place fabric pieces together. Sew along 2 long edges and 1 short edge; turn right side out. Press raw edges 1/4" to wrong side; press 1/4" to wrong side again. Insert mat board into case. To close, stitch along fold.

B.Y.O.B.
(Bring Your Own Bag)

Finished Size:
18"w x 14½"h x 4½"d (46 cm x 37 cm x 11 cm)

SHOPPING LIST

Yardage is based on 43"/44" (109 cm/112 cm) wide fabric with a usable width of 40" (102 cm).

☐ ¼ yd (23 cm) of small dot print fabric #1 for letter background and button background

☐ ⅛ yd (11 cm) of red mottled print fabric #2 for inside letter frame

☐ 1¾ yds (1.6 m) of large dot print fabric #3 for letter, outside letter frame, narrow vertical strips, sides, bottom, handles, lining, and inside pockets

☐ ½ yd (46 cm) of large floral print fabric #4 for bag front and back

☐ 1⅝ yds (1.5 m) of 44"/45" (112 cm x 114 cm) wide single-sided fusible fleece (such as The Warm Company® Warm Fleece™ or Pellon® #987F)

☐ Four 1½" (38 mm) buttons

☐ Paper-backed fusible web

☐ Stabilizer

☐ Water-soluble fabric marking pen

CUTTING THE PIECES

*Follow **Rotary Cutting**, page 58, **Cutting Chart**, and **Cutting Diagrams**, to cut fabric. All measurements include ¹/₄" seam allowances.*

Cutting Chart

PIECE(S)	FABRIC	SIZE	CUT
1	#1	7¹/₂" x 7¹/₂"	1
2, 3	#2	1" x 7¹/₂"	2
4, 5	#2	1" x 8¹/₂"	2
6, 7	#3	1" x 8¹/₂"	2
8, 9	#3	1" x 9¹/₂"	2
10	#4	5" x 9¹/₂"	1
11	#4	4¹/₂" x 14"	1
12	#4	2" x 14"	1
13	#4	1¹/₂" x 15"	1
14, 16	#3	1" x 15"	2
15	#1	3" x 15"	1
Front	Fusible fleece	18¹/₂" x 15"	1
Back	#4, Fusible fleece	18¹/₂" x 15"	1 each
Sides	#3, Fusible fleece	15" x 5"	2 each
Bottom	#3, Fusible fleece	18¹/₂" x 5"	1 each
Handles	#3, Fusible fleece	26" x 5"	2 each
Lining	#3, Fusible fleece	23" x 17¹/₄"	2 each
Inside Pockets	#3	23" x 12"	2
Inside Pocket	Fusible fleece	23" x 5¹/₂"	2

Fabric #3 Cutting Diagram

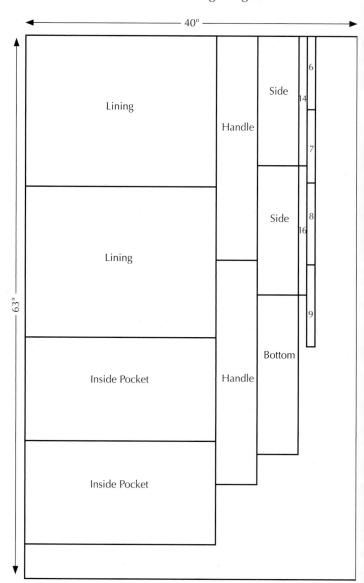

Fabric #4 Cutting Diagram

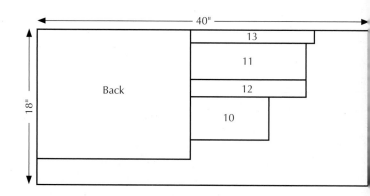

Fusible Fleece Cutting Diagram

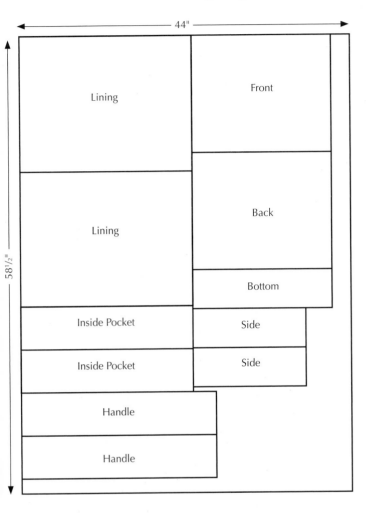

CUTTING THE APPLIQUÉS

From large dot print fabric #3:

• Find a font you like on the computer. Size desired letter to approximately 6" tall; print. Using printed letter for pattern, refer to **Preparing Fusible Appliqués**, page 60, to cut desired **letter**.

MAKING THE BAG FRONT

*Follow **Piecing**, page 59, and **Pressing**, page 60, to make bag. Match right sides and use ¼" seam allowances unless otherwise indicated.*

1. Center and fuse **letter** to **letter background**. Refer to **Satin Stitch Applique**, page 61, to stitch letter in place.
2. Refer to **Fig. 1** and sew pieces in the order shown to make the bag front. Bag front should measure 18½" x 15", including seam allowances.

Fig. 1

3. Place wrong side of bag front on fusible side of **fusible fleece front**. Follow manufacturer's instructions to fuse.
4. Quilt in the ditch along seamlines as desired.

MAKING THE BAG

1. Place the wrong side of the **back**, **sides**, and **bottom** on the fusible side of their respective **fusible fleece pieces**; fuse.
2. Sew bag sides to bag front, stopping ¼" from bottom.
3. Sew bag sides to bag back, stopping ¼" from bottom.
4. Sew bottom to bag front, back, and sides, stopping ¼" from each corner.
5. Trim the corners and turn the bag right side out.
6. Spacing the buttons about 3" apart, sew the buttons to the button background on the bag front.

MAKING AND ATTACHING THE HANDLES

1. Place the wrong side of 1 **handle** on the fusible side of 1 **fusible fleece handle**; fuse.
2. Matching **wrong** sides, press handle in half; unfold. Press long raw edges of handle to meet the center crease.
3. Matching folded edges, fold handle in half; press.
4. Pin edges together. Sewing through all layers, topstitch handle close to each edge. Sew additional topstitch lines if desired for a decorative effect.
5. Repeat Steps 1-4 for remaining handle.
6. Pin raw edges of 1 handle even with top edge and 5½" from side seams on right side of bag back **(Fig. 2)**; baste in place. Repeat for remaining handle on bag front.

Fig. 2

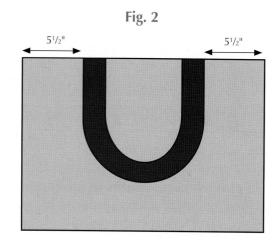

MAKING THE INSIDE POCKETS

1. Matching wrong sides, fold **inside pocket** in half lengthwise so that pocket is 23" x 6" .
2. Unfold the pocket and place the fusible side of the **fusible fleece inside pocket** on the wrong side of the fabric, aligning 1 long edge of the fleece with the fold of the fabric. Refold the pocket and fuse fleece in place.
3. Repeat Steps 1-2 for remaining inside pocket.

MAKING THE LINING

1. Place the wrong side of 1 **lining** on the fusible side of 1 **fusible fleece lining** and fuse.
2. Draw a horizontal line across lining 14" from 1 long edge of bag (top).
3. With folded edge of inside pocket pointing downward, match raw edges of pocket to drawn line **(Fig. 3)**; pin. Sew pocket in place ¼" from edge.

Fig. 3

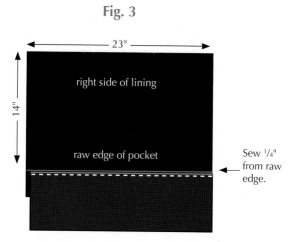

4. Press pocket up and baste at each side. Sew vertical lines to create pocket dividers **(Fig. 4)**.

Fig. 4

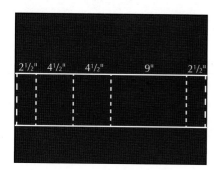

4. Refer to **Fig. 5** to cut a 2¼" notch from each bottom corner.

Fig. 5

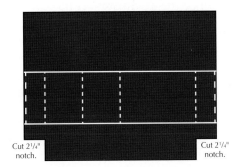

Cut 2¼" notch.

Cut 2¼" notch.

6. Repeat Steps 1–5 to make remaining lining piece.
7. Matching pockets and leaving a 6" opening for turning, sew lining pieces together along each side and the bottom *(Fig. 6)*.

Fig. 6

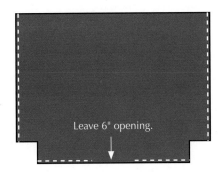

Leave 6" opening.

8. To box the bottom, match right sides and align side seams with bottom seam; sew across ends *(Fig. 7)*.

Fig. 7

ASSEMBLING THE BAG

1. Matching right sides, place the bag inside the lining with the handle sandwiched in between. Sew raw edges together around top *(Fig. 8)*.

Fig. 8

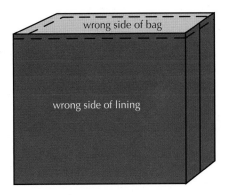

wrong side of bag

wrong side of lining

2. Turn bag right side out through opening in lining. Hand stitch opening closed. Push lining into bag. Topstitch around top of bag if desired.

OPTIONAL STURDY BOTTOM

Cut 2 pieces of mat board 4½" x 18"; glue together. Cut two 5½" x 19½" fabric pieces. Matching right sides, place fabric pieces together. Sew along 2 long edges and 1 short edge; turn right side out. Press raw edges ¼" to wrong side; press ¼" to wrong side again. Insert mat board into case. To hem edges, stitch along fold.

Messenger Bag

Jelly Rolls and Bali Pops are precut strips and are easy to use for this bag. You can also cut your own strips from fat quarters, fat eighths, twice the charms, or your scraps. The bag flap can be closed with a button and buttonhole or a magnetic snap.

Finished Size:
9"w x 9"h (23 cm x 23 cm)

SHOPPING LIST

Yardage is based on 43"/44" (109 cm/112 cm) wide fabric with a usable width of 40" (102 cm).

☐ Assorted strips 2$\frac{1}{8}$" to 2$\frac{7}{8}$" (5 cm to 7 cm) wide in varying lengths no less than 15" (38 cm) long

☐ $\frac{3}{8}$ yd (34 cm) of fabric #1 for strap, outside pocket, and flap

☐ $\frac{3}{8}$ yd (34 cm) of fabric #2 for lining and inside pockets

☐ $\frac{3}{8}$ yd (34 cm) of 44"/45" (112 cm/114 cm) wide single sided fusible fleece (such as The Warm Company® Warm Fleece™ or Pellon® #987F)

☐ Two $\frac{5}{8}$" (16 mm) buttons and two 1" (25 mm) buttons and 1 optional magnetic snap

☐ Water-soluble fabric marking pen

CUTTING THE PIECES

*Follow **Rotary Cutting**, page 58, and **Cutting Chart**, to cut fabric.*
All measurements include ¼" seam allowances.

Cutting Chart

PIECE	FABRIC	SIZE	CUT
strap	#1	2" x 40"	1
outside pocket	#1	pattern, page 56	2
flap	#1	pattern, page 56	2
lining	#2	pattern, page 54-55	2
inside pocket	#2	pattern, page 54-55	4
flap	fusible fleece	pattern, page 56	1
front/back	fusible fleece	10" x 10"	2
strap	fusible fleece	2" x 40"	1

MAKING THE BAG FRONT/BACK

*Follow **Piecing**, page 59, and **Pressing**, page 60, to make bag. Match right sides and use ¹/₄" seam allowances unless otherwise indicated.*

1. Draw a line across the fusible side of the **fusible fleece front** at approximately a 30° angle. The angle does not have to be exact.

2. With wrong side of fabric against fusible side of fleece, position 1 strip along line on fusible fleece front *(Fig. 1)*; pin.

Fig. 1

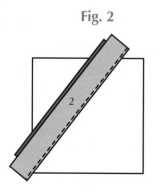

3. Matching right sides and raw edges, place a second strip on the previous strip; sew along the right edge *(Fig. 2)*. Flip second strip right side up *(Fig. 3)*; pin in place.

Fig. 2

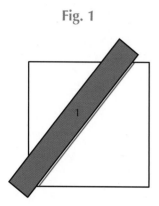

Fig. 3

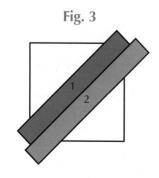

4. Matching right sides and raw edges, place a third strip on the previous strip; sew along the right edge *(Fig. 4)*. Flip third strip right side up *(Fig. 5)*; pin in place.

Fig. 4

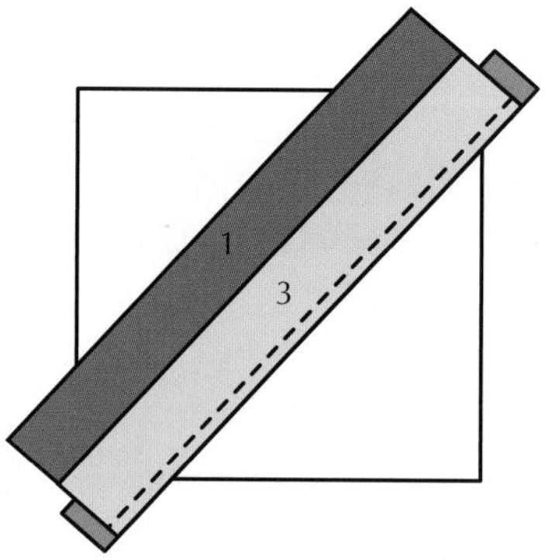

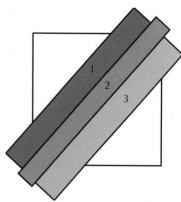

Fig. 5

5. Continue sewing strips in this manner until entire fleece front is covered. Follow manufacturer's instructions to fuse fabric to fleece.

6. Repeat Steps 1-5 to make back.

7. Use pattern, pages 54-55, to cut messenger bag front and back.

MAKING AND ATTACHING THE OUTSIDE POCKETS

1. Sew 2 **outside pockets** together leaving a small opening for turning. Clip seam allowances and turn right side out; press. Sew opening closed.

2. Press top of pocket down to form a flap as indicated on outside pocket pattern. Refer to **Fig. 6** to position pocket on bag front.

Fig. 6

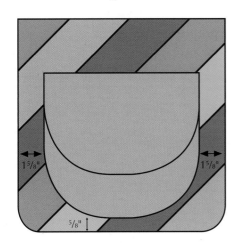

3. Folding flap up out of the way, topstitch edge of pocket from fold line to fold line.
4. Sew 1" button to pocket flap.

MAKING BAG LINING

1. Sew 2 **inside pocket** pieces together along straight edge. Press pocket right side out.
2. Matching curved edges, place inside pocket on **lining**; baste along raw edges.
3. Sew a vertical line down center of pocket.
4. Repeat Steps 1-3 for remaining pocket.
5. With pockets sandwiched in between, sew lining pieces together along curved raw edges.

MAKING THE STRAP

1. Place strap on fleece strap; fuse.
2. Matching right sides, sew strap together along 1 long side and 1 short side. Turn strap right side out. (***Note:*** *One short end is sewn just to make it easier to turn the strap. A small dowel or chopstick may be helpful for turning.*) Press strap.
3. Cut ¹⁄₂" off sewn short end of strap.

MAKING THE FLAP

1. Place wrong side of one **flap** on fusible side of **fusible fleece flap**; fuse. If using magnetic snap, attach one half of magnetic snap to fused flap as shown on pattern. Sew remaining 1" button to remaining flap as shown on pattern.
2. Sew flap pieces together along curved raw edges. Clip seam allowances, turn right sides out, and press. Baste straight edges closed.
3. Topstitch around curved edges.
4. If using buttonhole, make buttonhole as shown on pattern.

ASSEMBLING THE BAG

1. Matching right sides, sew bag front and bag back together along curved raw edges. Clip seam allowances and turn bag right side out.
2. Referring to **Fig. 7**, and aligning raw ends of strap with raw edge of bag, pin straps to bag back. Test "fit" before sewing. Adjust handle length to suit your personal taste. Baste in place.

Fig. 7

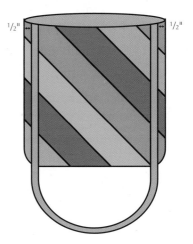

3. Matching right sides and straight raw edges and with handle sandwiched in between, pin flap to bag back. Flap should just fit between side seams. Sew in place.
4. Matching right sides and raw edges, place bag into lining with flap and handle sandwiched in between; pin. Leaving an opening for turning on back of bag, stitch around top.
5. Turn bag right side out. Push lining into bag. Hand stitch opening closed. Topstitch around top of bag.
6. Sew ⁵⁄₈" buttons to flap. Attach remaining half of magnetic snap or remaining 1" button to front.

Steps

The top of this bag folds to the outside to form a cuff, allowing the lining to show. We give 2 options for lining the bag. The bag can be lined using 2 fat quarters, as shown in the blue/pink/red version, right, or with strips, as shown in the purple version, page 45.

Finished Size:
14"w x 11½"h x 4½"d (36 cm x 29 cm x 11 cm)

SHOPPING LIST

Fabric yardage is based on 43"/44" (109 cm/112 cm) wide fabric with a usable width of 40" (102 cm). Fat quarters must measure at least 21" x 18" (53 cm x 46 cm). Charm squares measure 5" x 5" (13 cm x 13 cm). Wof refers to width of fabric.

- ☐ 2 assorted fat quarters for bag body
- ☐ 1 fat quarter for outside pocket lining and optional loop closure (shown on blue/pink/red version)
- ☐ 1⅝ yds (1.5 m) of single-sided fusible fleece (such as Pellon® 987F)
- ☐ Assorted buttons - 14 for pockets, 6-12 for cuff, and 2 for sides
- ☐ 1½ yds (1.4 m) of jumbo rickrack (optional)
- ☐ Water-soluble fabric marking pen

For fat quarter and charm square version (shown in blues, pinks, and reds), you will also need:

- ☐ Two assorted fat quarters for lining
- ☐ 25 charm squares for handles and outside pockets
- ☐ Two assorted fat quarters for inside pockets

For fat quarter and strip version (shown in purples), you will also need:

- ☐ 20 strips 2½"w (6 cm) x wof for handles, lining, and outside pocket
- ☐ ⅜ yd (34 cm) of fabric #1 for inside pockets

CUTTING THE PIECES

Follow Rotary Cutting, page 58, and Cutting Charts, to cut fabric. All measurements include ¹/₄" seam allowances.

Cutting Chart (for either version)

PIECE(S)	FABRIC	SIZE	CUT
bag body	2 assorted fat quarters	10¹/₂" x 18"	4
outside pocket lining	fat quarter	pattern, page 57	2
loop closure (optional)	fat quarter	1" x 14¹/₂"	1
handle	fusible fleece	2¹/₂" x 36¹/₂"	2
bag body	fusible fleece	20¹/₂" x 35¹/₂"	1
lining	fusible fleece	20¹/₂" x 18"	2
inside pocket	fusible fleece	20¹/₂" x 5¹/₂"	2
outside pocket lining*	fusible fleece	pattern, page 57	2

*trim ¹/₂" from bottom as shown on pattern

Cutting Chart (for fat quarter and charm square version)

lining	2 assorted fat quarters	10¹/₂" x 18"	2 from each
handles and outside pocket rectangles	charm squares	2¹/₂" x 5"	50
inside pockets	2 assorted fat quarters	20¹/₂" x 12"	1 from each

Cutting Chart (for fat quarter and strip version)

handles	strips	2¹/₂" x 36¹/₂"	4
lining	strips	2¹/₂" x 18"	20
outside pocket rectangles	strips	2¹/₂" x 5"	18
inside pockets	fabric #1	20¹/₂" x 12"	2

MAKING THE OUTSIDE POCKETS

Follow Piecing, page 59, and Pressing, page 60, to make the bag. Match right sides and use ¹/₄" seam allowances unless otherwise indicated.

1. Sew 3 assorted 2¹/₂" x 5" **rectangles** together to make **Unit 1**. Make 4 Unit 1's.

Unit 1 (make 4)

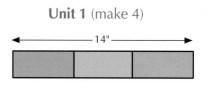

2. Sew 2 assorted 2¹/₂" x 5" rectangles together to make **Unit 2**. Make 2 Unit 2's.

Unit 2 (make 2)

3. Sew 2 Unit 1's, 1 Unit 2, and 1 rectangle together to make **outside pocket**. Press seam allowances up. Make 2 outside pockets.

Outside Pocket (make 2)

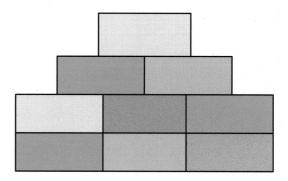

4. With long edge of fleece ½" above long edge of pocket lining, follow manufacturer's instructions and fuse the wrong side of **outside pocket lining** on the fusible side of **fusible fleece outside pocket lining**.

5. Leaving long edges (bottom) open, sew outside pocket to **outside pocket lining** around remaining edges *(Fig. 1)*.

6. Trim outside corners; clip inside corners *(Fig. 2)*. Turn pocket right side out; press.

Fig. 1

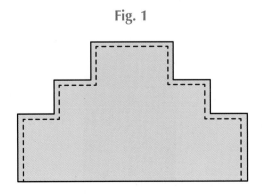

Fig. 2

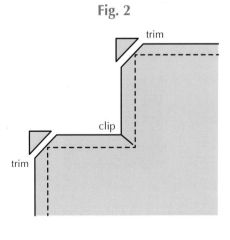

7. Draw a line down the center of pocket *(Fig. 3)*.

Fig. 3

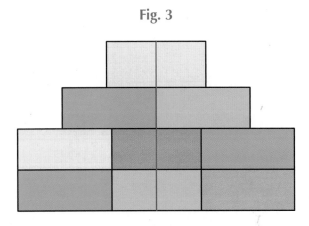

8. Topstitch ¼" from top and side edges *(Fig. 4)*.

Fig. 4

9. Repeat Steps 4-8 to make remaining pocket.

MAKING THE BAG BODY

1. Sew 2 **bag body** pieces together to make **Unit 3**. Make 2 Unit 3's.

Unit 3 (make 2)

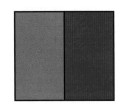

2. Sew 2 Unit 3's together to make **Bag Body**.

Bag Body

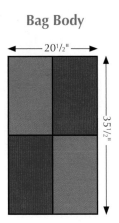
20½"
35½"

3. Fuse the wrong side of the bag body on the fusible side of **fusible fleece bag body**.

4. Draw a line 2¾" from each side of short seamline *(Fig. 5)*.

Fig. 5

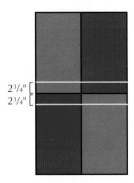
2¾"
2¾"

5. Aligning raw edge with drawn line, center right side of 1 pocket on right side of bag body. Sew ¼" from line *(Fig. 6)*.

Fig. 6

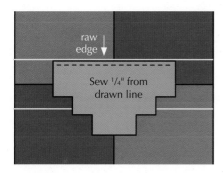

6. Press pocket up. Topstitch across top and sides, leaving "steps" open and along drawn line *(Fig. 7)*.

Fig. 7

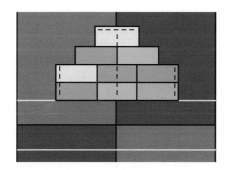

7. Repeat Steps 5-6 to attach remaining pocket to opposite end of bag body.
8. Sew buttons to pockets as desired.
9. Matching right sides and short edges, fold bag body in half. Sew along side edges. Turn bag body right side out.
10. To box bottom, match wrong sides and align side seam with bottom seam. Refer to **Fig. 8** to sew across point 2½" from tip. Topstitch along pointed edges.

Fig. 8

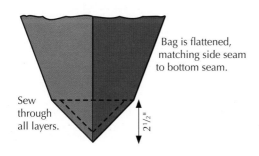

11. Fold triangle up *(Fig. 9)*. Sewing through all layers, sew a button to triangle.

Fig. 9

fold triangle up

12. Repeat Steps 10-11 to box remaining side seam and bottom seam.

MAKING THE LINING AND INSIDE POCKETS

1. **For lining using pieces cut from fat quarters**, sew 2 **lining pieces** together to make **Unit 4**. Make 2 Unit 4's.

Unit 4 (make 2)

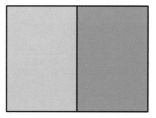

For lining using strips, sew 10 **lining strips** together to make **Unit 5**. Make 2 Unit 5's.

Unit 5 (make 2)

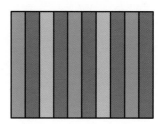

2. Fuse the wrong side of Unit 4 or 5 on the fusible side of **fusible fleece lining** to make **lining**. Make 2 linings.

3. Draw a horizontal line across right side of lining 3¹/₄" from bottom edge *(Fig. 10)*.

Fig. 10

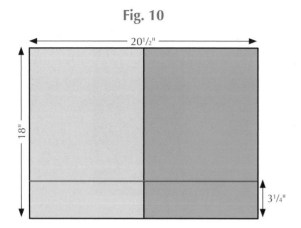

4. Matching **wrong** sides and long edges, fold **inside pocket** in half; press.

5. Open inside pocket and place fusible fleece against fold on wrong side of fabric. Close inside pocket; fuse fleece in place.

6. Repeat Steps 3-5 to make remaining inside pocket.

7. With folded edge of inside pocket pointing downward, match raw edges of pocket to drawn line *(Fig. 11)*; pin. Sew pocket in place ¹/₄" from raw edges.

Fig. 11

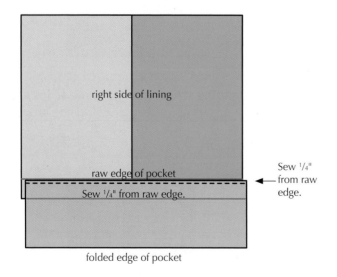

8. Press pocket up and baste at sides.

9. Sew vertical lines to create pocket dividers. Cut a 2¹/₂" notch in each bottom corner *(Fig. 12)*.

Fig. 12

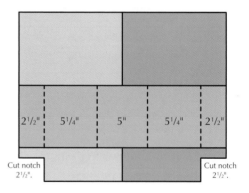

10. Repeat Steps 7-9 for remaining lining and pocket.

11. Matching pockets and leaving a 6" opening for turning, sew lining pieces together along each side and bottom *(Fig. 13)*.

Fig. 13

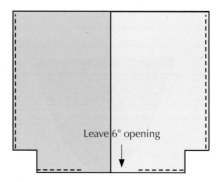

2. To box bottom, match right sides and align side seam with bottom seam; sew across ends *(Fig. 14)*.

Fig. 14

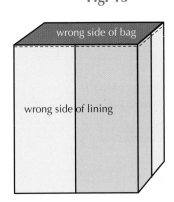

ASSEMBLING THE BAG

1. Matching right sides, place bag body into lining. Aligning top raw edges, stitch around top *(Fig. 15)*.

Fig. 15

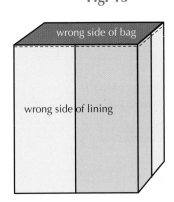

2. Turn bag right side out through the opening in the lining. Hand stitch opening closed. Tuck lining into bag. Topstitch around top of bag.

MAKING AND ATTACHING THE HANDLES

1. If using charm square handles, match short ends and sew 8 assorted 2¹/₂" x 5" fabric pieces together to make a 36¹/₂" long handle. Repeat to make a total of 4 handles.

2. Using charm square handle or strip handle, fuse the wrong side of 1 handle on the fusible side of 1 **fusible fleece handle**. Repeat with remaining fusible fleece handle.

3. Leaving a 3" opening along 1 long side, sew 1 **handle** and one fleece-fused handle together along all edges. Trim corners and turn handle right side out; press. Hand stitch opening closed. Repeat to make remaining handle.

4. Topstitch ¹/₄" from all edges of each handle.

5. Turn bag wrong side out. With inside edges about 3" from center of bag and bottom edges about 5" from top of bag, pin handle ends to lining of bag. Test "fit" before sewing, adjusting handle placement as desired. Sew handles in place as shown in **Fig. 16**. Turn bag right side out.

Fig. 16

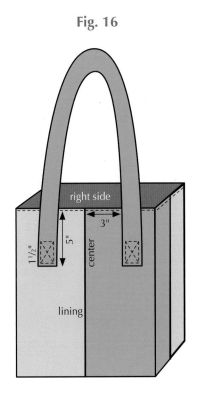

EMBELLISHING THE BAG

1. Fold the lining to the outside about 3" to form a cuff.

2. If desired, sew rickrack to cuff with center of rickrack about 1¹/₄" from edge.

3. Sew buttons to cuff as desired.

For Optional Loop Closure:
Matching wrong sides, press loop closure in half; unfold. Press long raw edges of closure to meet the center crease. Matching folded edges, fold closure in half; press. Pin edges together. Sewing through all layers, sew closure close to each long edge. Fold closure in half and sew ends inside bag at center back, below fold of cuff. If desired, use a Satin Stitch (see page 61) to cover raw ends.

The Big Easy

Patterns

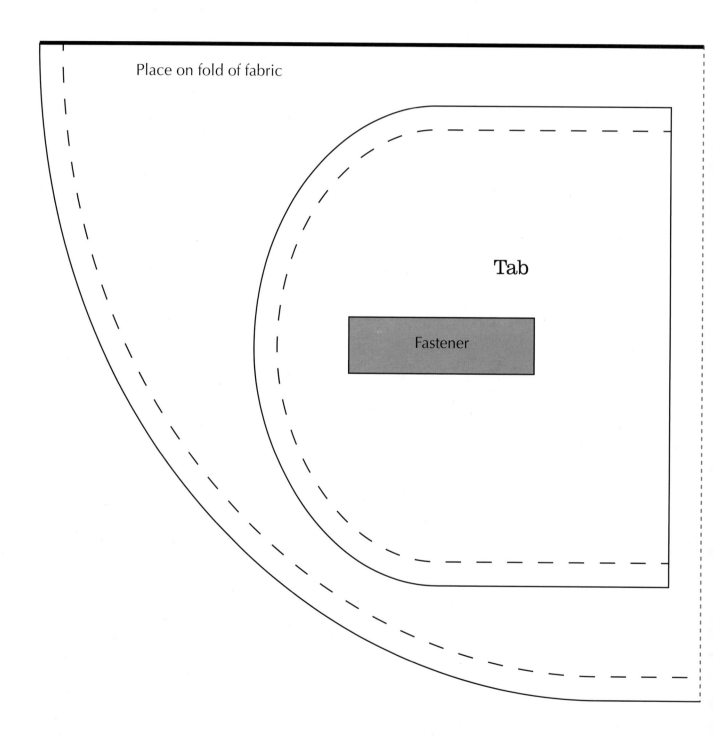

Place on fold of fabric

Tab

Fastener

Place on fold of fabric

End/End Lining

To trace a complete pattern,
match red dashed lines.

Snap Placement

○

The Big Shopper
Pattern

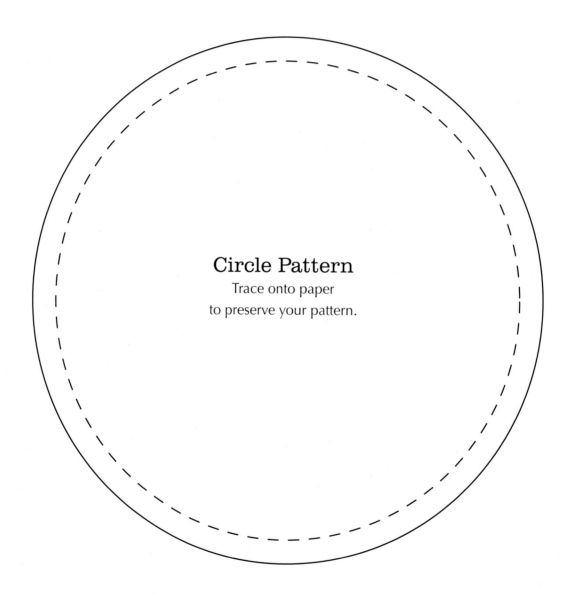

Circle Pattern
Trace onto paper
to preserve your pattern.

Messenger Bag
Patterns

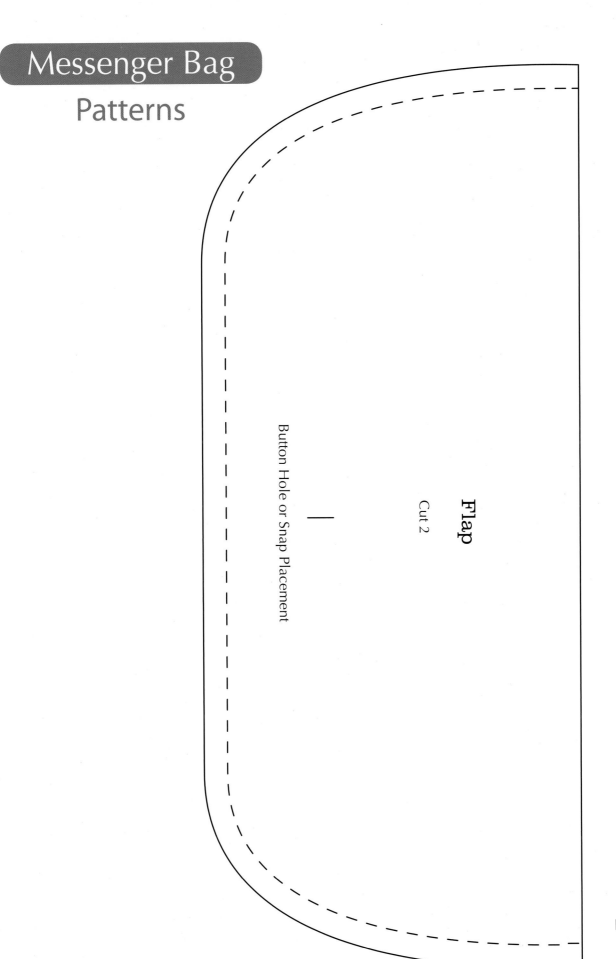

Button Hole or Snap Placement

Flap

Cut 2

Patterns continue
on page 52

Messenger Bag
Patterns

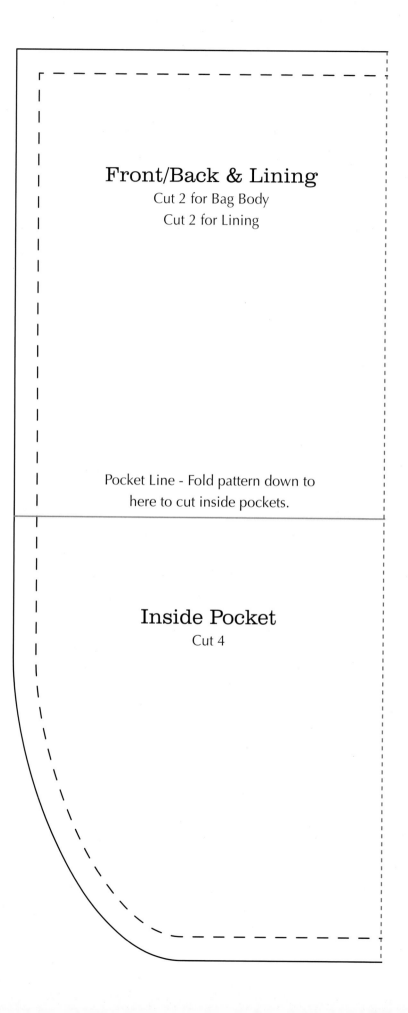

Front/Back & Lining

Cut 2 for Bag Body

Cut 2 for Lining

Pocket Line - Fold pattern down to here to cut inside pockets.

Inside Pocket

Cut 4

Front/Back & Lining
Cut 2 for Bag Body
Cut 2 for Lining

To trace a complete patterns,
match red dashed lines.

Pocket Line - Fold pattern down
to here to cut inside pockets.

Inside Pocket
Cut 4

Patterns continue
on page 56

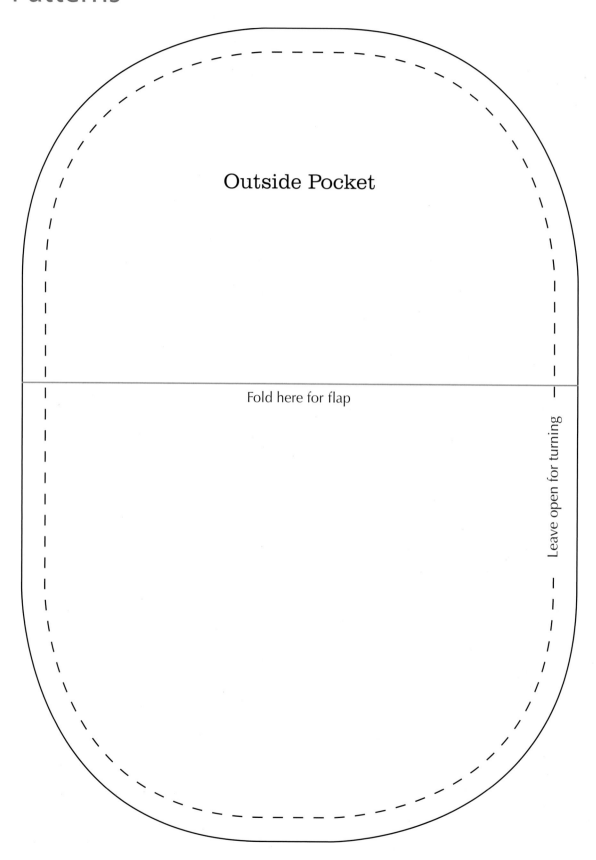

Outside Pocket

Fold here for flap

Leave open for turning

Patterns

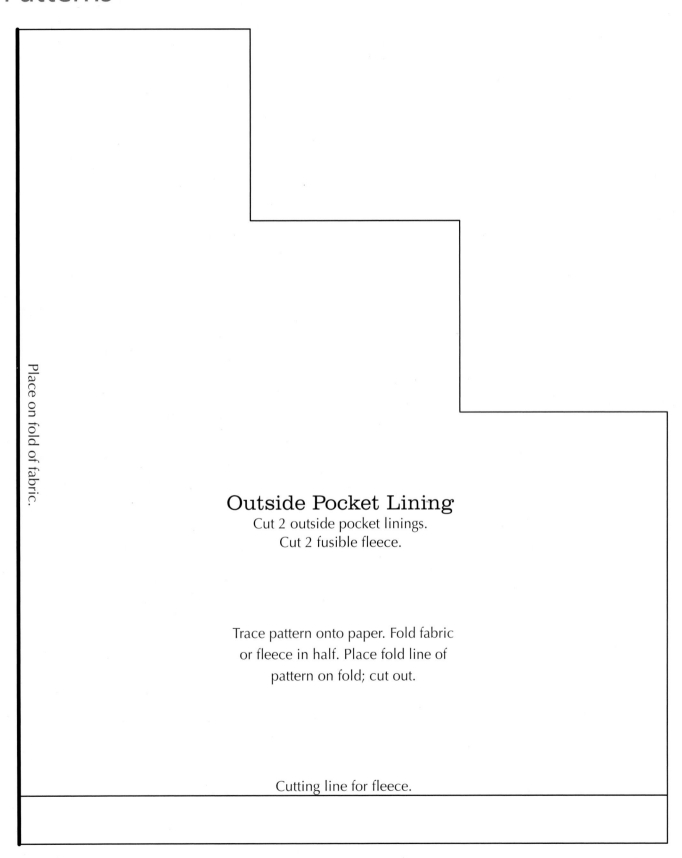

Place on fold of fabric.

Outside Pocket Lining
Cut 2 outside pocket linings.
Cut 2 fusible fleece.

Trace pattern onto paper. Fold fabric
or fleece in half. Place fold line of
pattern on fold; cut out.

Cutting line for fleece.

General Instructions

To make your sewing easier and more enjoyable, we encourage you to carefully read all of the general instructions, study the color photographs, and familiarize yourself with the individual project instructions before beginning a project.

FABRICS

SELECTING FABRICS

Choose high-quality, medium-weight 100% cotton fabrics. All-cotton fabrics hold a crease better, and fray less.

Yardage requirements listed for each project are based on 43"/44" wide fabric with a "usable" width of 40" after shrinkage and trimming selvages. Actual usable width will probably vary slightly from fabric to fabric. Our recommended yardage lengths should be adequate for occasional re-squaring of fabric when many cuts are required.

PREPARING FABRICS

Pre-washing fabrics may cause edges to ravel. As a result, your pre-cut fabric pieces may not be large enough to cut all of the pieces required for your chosen project. Therefore, we do not recommend pre-washing your yardage or pre-cut fabrics.

Before cutting, prepare fabrics with a steam iron set on cotton and starch or sizing. The starch or sizing will give the fabric a crisp finish. This will make cutting more accurate and may make piecing easier.

ROTARY CUTTING

CUTTING FROM YARDAGE

- Place fabric on work surface with fold closest to you.

- Cut all strips from the selvage-to-selvage width of the fabric unless otherwise indicated in project instructions.

- Square left edge of fabric using rotary cutter and rulers (*Figs. 1-2*).

Fig. 1

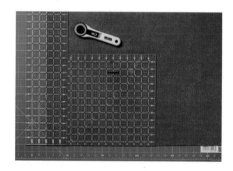

Fig. 2

• To cut each strip required for a project, place ruler over cut edge of fabric, aligning desired marking on ruler with cut edge; make cut *(Fig. 3)*.

Fig. 3

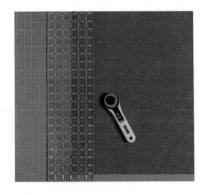

• When cutting several strips from a single piece of fabric, it is important to make sure that cuts remain at a perfect right angle to the fold; square fabric as needed.

CUTTING FROM FAT QUARTERS

• Place fabric flat on work surface with short edge closest to you.

• Cut all strips parallel to the long edge of the fabric in the same manner as cutting from yardage.

• To cut each strip required for a project, place ruler over cut edge of fabric, aligning desired marking on ruler with cut edge; make cut.

PIECING

Precise cutting, followed by accurate piecing, will ensure that all pieces of quilt top fit together well.

• Set sewing machine stitch length for approximately 11 stitches per inch.

• Use neutral-colored general-purpose sewing thread (not quilting thread) in needle and in bobbin.

• An accurate 1/4" seam allowance is *essential*. Presser feet that are 1/4" wide are available for most sewing machines.

• When piecing, always place pieces right sides together and match raw edges; pin if necessary.

• Trim away points of seam allowances that extend beyond edges of sewn pieces.

SEWING ACROSS SEAM INTERSECTIONS

When sewing across the intersection of two seams, place pieces right sides together and match seams exactly, making sure seam allowances are pressed in opposite directions *(Fig. 4)*.

Fig. 4

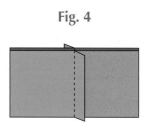

SEWING SHARP POINTS

To ensure sharp points when joining triangular or diagonal pieces, stitch across the center of the "X" (shown in pink) formed on wrong side by previous seams *(Fig. 5)*.

Fig. 5

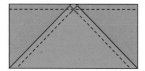

PRESSING

• Use steam iron set on "Cotton" for all pressing.

• Press after sewing each seam.

• Seam allowances are almost always pressed to one side, usually toward the darker fabric. However, to reduce bulk it may occasionally be necessary to press seam allowances toward the lighter fabric or even to press them open.

• To prevent a dark fabric seam allowance from showing through a light fabric, trim the darker seam allowance slightly narrower than the lighter seam allowance.

• To press long seams, such as those in long strip sets, without curving or other distortion, lay strips across width of the ironing board.

• When sewing squares or rectangles into rows, seam allowances may be pressed in one direction in odd numbered rows and in the opposite direction in even numbered rows. When sewing rows together, press seam allowances in one direction.

MACHINE APPLIQUÉ
PREPARING FUSIBLE APPLIQUÉS

White or light-colored fabrics may need to be lined with fusible interfacing before applying fusible web to prevent darker fabrics from showing through.

1. Place paper-backed fusible web, paper side up, over appliqué pattern. Trace pattern onto paper side of web with pencil as many times as indicated in project instructions for a single fabric.

2. Follow manufacturer's instructions to fuse traced patterns to wrong side of fabrics. Do not remove paper backing.

3. Use scissors to cut out appliqué pieces along traced lines. Remove paper backing from all pieces.

SATIN STITCH APPLIQUÉ

A good satin stitch is a thick, smooth, almost solid line of zigzag stitching that covers the exposed raw edges of appliqué pieces.

1. Pin stabilizer, such as paper or any of the commercially available products, on wrong side of background fabric before stitching appliqués in place.

2. Thread sewing machine with general-purpose thread; use general-purpose thread that matches background fabric in bobbin.

3. Set sewing machine for a medium (approximately $1/8$") zigzag stitch and a short stitch length. Slightly loosening the top tension may yield a smoother stitch.

4. Begin by stitching two or three stitches in place (drop feed dogs or set stitch length at 0) to anchor thread. Most of the Satin Stitch should be on the appliqué with the right edge of the stitch falling at the outside edge of the appliqué. Stitch over all exposed raw edges of appliqué pieces.

5. (**Note:** Dots on **Figs. 6-11** indicate where to leave needle in fabric when pivoting.) For outside corners, stitch just past corner, stopping with needle in background fabric **(Fig. 6)**. Raise presser foot. Pivot project, lower presser foot, and stitch adjacent side **(Fig. 7)**.

Fig. 6   **Fig. 7**

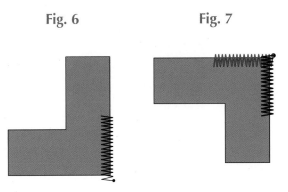

6. For inside corners, stitch just past corner, stopping with needle in appliqué fabric **(Fig. 8)**. Raise presser foot. Pivot project, lower presser foot, and stitch adjacent side **(Fig. 9)**.

Fig. 8   **Fig. 9**

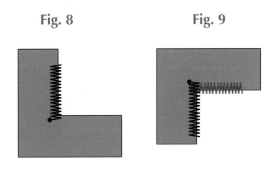

7. When stitching outside curves, stop with needle in background fabric. Raise presser foot and pivot project as needed. Lower presser foot and continue stitching, pivoting as often as necessary to follow curve **(Fig. 10)**.

Fig. 10

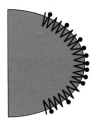

8. When stitching inside curves, stop with needle in appliqué fabric. Raise presser foot and pivot project as needed. Lower presser foot and continue stitching, pivoting as often as necessary to follow curve (*Fig. 11*).

Fig. 11

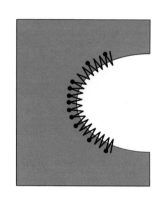

9. Do not backstitch at end of stitching. Pull threads to wrong side of background fabric; knot thread and trim ends.
10. Carefully tear away stabilizer.

BLANKET STITCH APPLIQUÉ

Some sewing machines are capable of a Blanket Stitch. Refer to your owner's manual for machine set-up. If your machine does not have this stitch, try any of the decorative stitches your machine has until you are satisfied with the look.

1. Thread sewing machine and bobbin with 100% cotton thread in desired weight.
2. Attach an open-toe presser foot. Select far right needle position and needle down (if your machine has these features).

3. If desired, pin a stabilizer, such as paper or any of the commercially available products on wrong side of background fabric before stitching appliqués in place.
4. Bring bobbin thread to the top of the fabric by lowering then raising the needle, bringing up the bobbin thread loop. Pull the loop all the way to the surface.
5. Begin by stitching two or three stitches in place (drop feed dogs or set stitch length at 0), or use your machine's lock stitch feature, if equipped, to anchor thread. Return setting to selected Blanket Stitch.
6. Most of the Blanket Stitch should be on the appliqué with the right edges of the stitch falling at the very outside edge of the appliqué. Stitch over all exposed raw edges of appliqué pieces.
7. (***Note:*** *Dots on* **Figs. 12-17** *indicate where to leave needle in fabric when pivoting.*) Always stopping with needle down in background fabric, refer to **Fig. 12** to stitch outside points like tips of leaves. Stop one stitch short of point. Raise presser foot. Pivot project slightly, lower presser foot, and make an angled Stitch 1. Take next stitch, stop at point, and pivot so Stitch 2 will be perpendicular to point. Pivot slightly to make Stitch 3. Continue stitching.

Fig. 12

8. For outside corners *(Fig. 13)*, stitch to corner, stopping with needle in background fabric. Raise presser foot. Pivot project, lower presser foot, and take an angled stitch. Raise presser foot. Pivot project, lower presser foot and stitch adjacent side.

Fig. 13

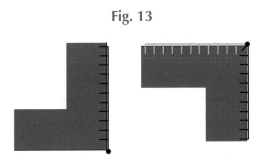

9. For inside corners *(Fig. 14)*, stitch to the corner, taking the last bite at corner and stopping with the needle down in background fabric. Raise presser foot. Pivot project, lower presser foot, and take an angled stitch. Raise presser foot. Pivot project, lower presser foot and stitch adjacent side.

Fig. 14

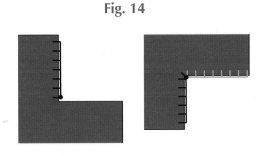

10. When stitching outside curves *(Fig. 15)*, stop with needle down in background fabric. Raise presser foot and pivot project as needed. Lower presser foot and continue stitching, pivoting as often as necessary to follow curve. Small circles may require pivoting between each stitch.

Fig. 15

11. When stitching inside curves *(Fig. 16)*, stop with needle down in background fabric. Raise presser foot and pivot project as needed. Lower presser foot and continue stitching, pivoting as often as necessary to follow curve.

Fig. 16

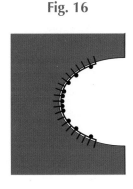

12. When stopping stitching, use a lock stitch to sew 5 or 6 stitches in place or use a needle to pull threads to wrong side of background fabric *(Fig. 17)*; knot, then trim ends.

Fig. 17

13. Carefully tear away stabilizer, if used.

QUILTING
TYPES OF QUILTING DESIGNS
In the Ditch Quilting
Quilting along seamlines or along edges of appliquéd pieces is called "in the ditch" quilting. This type of quilting should be done on side **opposite** seam allowance and does not have to be marked.

Outline Quilting
Quilting a consistent distance, usually $1/4$", from seam or appliqué is called "outline" quilting. Outline quilting may be marked, or $1/4$" masking tape may be placed along seamlines for quilting guide. (Do not leave tape on quilt longer than necessary, since it may leave an adhesive residue.)

MACHINE QUILTING
Use general-purpose thread in bobbin. Do not use quilting thread. Thread the needle of machine with general-purpose thread or transparent monofilament thread to make quilting blend with quilt top fabrics. Use decorative thread, such as a metallic or contrasting-color general-purpose thread, to make quilting lines stand out more.

1. Set stitch length for six to ten stitches per inch and attach a walking foot to sewing machine.

2. Begin stitching, using very short stitches for the first $1/4$" to "lock" quilting. Stitch using one hand on each side of walking foot to slightly spread fabric and to guide fabric through machine. Lock stitches at end of quilting line.

Metric Conversion Chart					
Inches x 2.54 = centimeters (cm)			Yards x .9144 = meters (m)		
Inches x 25.4 = millimeters (mm)			Yards x 91.44 = centimeters (cm)		
Inches x .0254 = meters (m)			Centimeters x .3937 = inches (")		
			Meters x 1.0936 = yards (yd)		
Standard Equivalents					
$1/8$"	3.2 mm	0.32 cm	$1/8$ yard	11.43 cm	0.11 m
$1/4$"	6.35 mm	0.635 cm	$1/4$ yard	22.86 cm	0.23 m
$3/8$"	9.5 mm	0.95 cm	$3/8$ yard	34.29 cm	0.34 m
$1/2$"	12.7 mm	1.27 cm	$1/2$ yard	45.72 cm	0.46 m
$5/8$"	15.9 mm	1.59 cm	$5/8$ yard	57.15 cm	0.57 m
$3/4$"	19.1 mm	1.91 cm	$3/4$ yard	68.58 cm	0.69 m
$7/8$"	22.2 mm	2.22 cm	$7/8$ yard	80 cm	0.8 m
1"	25.4 mm	2.54 cm	1 yard	91.44 cm	0.91 m